Hope

Versus

Faith

Hope

Versus

Faith

*Practical Applications
of The Spiritual Weapons
of The Mind and Heart*

REV. EMIL ELORM CLAD

Copyright ©2021 Rev. Emil Elorm Clad

ISBN: Paperback   978-9988-2-7004-9
            E-book   9988-2-7004-6

Published By:
CToG Media Group
+233 20 842 9790
+233 20 030 1423

E-mail:
emilclad@yahoo.com

Editors:
Rev. Emil Elorm Clad
Mr. Elvis Gota

Assistant Editors:
Mr. Selorm Adonoo
Mr. Emmanuel Acquah Sawyerr
Miss Keziah Eyram Clad

Layout & Cover Artists:
Roland Bruce
Godwin Attipoe
Selorm Gbormitta

Dedication

To the Precious

Holy Spirit

My Lord, My God,
My Teacher, My Guide,
My Eternal Inheritance,
My Present Help in Time of Need...
Thank You Very Much.

Acknowledgments

I give glory to God for the faith series. I have always desired to compile the teachings into a book but could not get it done all this while.

My dear cousin, Bishop Phillips Banini, has become increasingly helpful in various aspects of my personal life and ministry in recent times. He actually brought up the idea of writing a second edition as well as improving on the cover design. I very much appreciate your invaluable contribution.

My gratitude also goes to God for blessing me with such great and resourceful personnel of the Christ Tower of Grace Media Group, including Christian Agbalekpor, David Agbesinyale, Emmanuel Sawyerr, Kojo Ocran, Paul Kelvin Kwame Dzakpasu, Kwame Owusu-Ansah, Roland Bruce, Samuel Elorm Agbesinyale, Selorm Adonoo and Selorm Gbormitta. The "Faith Series" cover design you showed me that Sunday after church service inspired me to start putting the materials together for this book.

I duly recognize the priceless contributions of my dear sons in ministry; Mr. Selorm Adonoo, and Emmanuel Sawyerr for the initial editing, proofreading and very helpful suggestions.

My unreserved appreciation goes to my dear brother and friend, Mr. Elvis Gota, for the kind gesture of final editing of the manuscript. That was quite a task by all standards. I cannot imagine how much work I pile on you from time to time. I owe you so much I cannot pay.

Can I ever thank the entire Christ Tower of Grace ministry Worldwide enough for what they mean to me and do for me? May God honor our Pastoral Team led by Pastor Charles Avornyo. Your encouragement spurs me on to strive for excellence.

My dear wife, Erica, and our precious children, Kemuel, Keziah, Keren, Kaila, and Ruby; your availability, love and support enables me to pursue the call. What a blessed family you all are to me. I am very grateful.

ENDORSEMENTS:

"I have truly enjoyed the depth of knowledge after reading this book. It is truly a revelation and a study material, biblically researched, very informative and great for small groups' studies. This is another great book! It is truly a must-read."

Bishop P.E. Banini
Phillips Banini Ministries,
Phoenix, Arizona, USA.

"*Hope Versus Faith* is extremely practical and perfect for discipleship classes. The expositions in the book are excellent and incredibly insightful. If you are longing to deepen your faith and take it to a completely new level, then this is the book for you! Meditate on the teachings within and your life will be transformed!"

Judy Coventry,
President, Mercy Triumphs Worldwide,
Author of *The Trading Floors, and Mastering the Trading*

Floors.
Goodyear, Arizona, USA.

"A masterful work of love by Rev. Emil Clad. Given the haziness and obfuscations related to this area of scripture, this book brings invaluable revelatory truth and spiritual harvest of redemptive insights that excite, challenge and empower the reader to live a fulfilled victorious Christian life. This book is a must for all libraries of faith and an excellent resource for equipping believers in the body of Christ."

Rev. Samuel Owusu-Bempah
Snr. Pastor and District Supervising Minister,
ICGC Prayer Temple, Kumasi, Ghana.

"For anyone seeking in-depth understanding of the subject, *Hope Versus Faith* is potentially the most informative book out there. It throws enormous light on the fine lines between "Hope", "Belief" and "Faith." Well thought out, well researched, good study material. Certainly a must-read."

Elvis Gota,
Mineral Exploration Geoscientist,

Minister of the gospel, Action Chapel International, Accra, Ghana.

"The ability to communicate difficult topics in the simplest of ways with few words is a great challenge for many teachers and authors. This book overcomes that challenge. It takes the difficult topics of hope and faith and makes them very easy to differentiate, understand, and apply. Not only is it a great read for the Pastor who seeks to teach his congregation these two core pillars of the Christian faith but it is also necessary for the everyday Christian who seeks to properly enact faith to please God and to persist in the hope of glory. I really enjoyed reading it and highly recommend it."

Emmanuel Sawyer,
PhD Researcher, University of Westminster,
London, UK.

"The subject of Faith is fundamental to the Christian walk. Without it, we cannot please God. Despite its importance, it is often one of the most ill-defined concepts. It becomes even more confounding when taught together with Hope. In *Hope versus Faith*, Rev.

Clad with precision, demystifies the two subjects and even proceeds to compare them, drawing important similarities and differences. Most crucially, he takes the reader on a journey of how to combine hope and faith, and tells how deploying the two produces results for effective Christian living. *Hope Versus Faith* is an incredibly easy-to-read reference material and a practical guide to a fulfilled life. It is a must-read. It is life-changing!"

Selorm Adonoo,
A Private Legal Practitioner
Talk Show Host,
Citi FM, Accra, Ghana.

INTRODUCTION

Faith is a very broad subject with many facets. Its doctrine is fundamental to life because it is the key to accessing God's grace, and the means to a victorious living. Without faith, it is NOT POSSIBLE to please God.

The passage does not say, "…it is difficult…" It says, "…it is impossible." That simply means faith is man's ability to please God. Without it, no one would be able to fulfil His standard of righteousness.

For these and many other reasons, we must consider the topic systematically and holistically. One way to achieve this is to compare and contrast it with other themes where they overlap. For instance, *hope* and *faith* have similarities and differences that are worthy of note.

Having been dissatisfied with the jargons that often characterize Christian literature, it has always been my passion to present simple and straightforward information for easy reading and in-depth understanding. This will help generate conviction and inspire many to pursue the course that ensures the certainty of success in life.

The content of this book is a series of messages on faith, which the author delivered in church. It has cleared up a major uncertainty surrounding the subject, renewed the minds of attendees and brought a paradigm shift in their perspectives.

One later wrote, *"The messages were awesome. I cannot quantify how blessed my life has been because of the series. I now see things differently…"* A similar experience comes your way through this medium.

Table of Contents

CHAPTER 1

The Three Important Virtues

"And now these three remain: faith, hope and love. But the greatest of these is love"
(1 Corinthians 13:13; NIV).

I was one of the two hundred and forty nine (249) privileged participants from Ghana who attended the August 2000 International Conference for Itinerant Evangelists in Amsterdam, Rai. It was sponsored by the Billy Graham Evangelistic Association (BGEA).

Interestingly, when I had the opportunity, I did not have a passport to acquire the necessary entry visa. Moreover, to process a valid passport, I had to submit my birth certificate among other requirements. The birth certificate in addition to the other documents aided in my acquisition of a passport with which I eventually obtained the visa to travel.

As equally important as all the three main documents were to my travel plans, I obtained them in a specific order – first, the birth certificate, and then the passport, followed by the visa acquisition. A fourth important element was the air ticket.

A few weeks before we travelled, I met a pastor of middle age who recounted how he also had the invitation to participate in the same conference. Unfortunately, he did not attempt to pursue it on the basis that he could not afford the cost of the air ticket.

That certainly startled me because I did not concern myself with the cost of travel at first. All my attention was on getting the documents one at a time. It was only during the process that I discovered all expenses were paid including air ticket.

However, here was someone who failed to organize himself and prepare, which is why he missed such a rare opportunity. Indeed, he made a grave mistake by putting the cart before the horse and blowing away the unique chance.

The above story demonstrates how different people handle the issue of faith differently depending on their individual viewpoints. In order to make the most out of the subject, we must appreciate and align with the sequence in which it occurs.

Three Important Virtues

There are three extremely important virtues in life. They are faith, hope and love. All three remain; meaning, they continue in their state without changing. We find the superlative word "greatest" connected to the virtue of love in the above passage. Hence, love is the greatest of all three.

However, there must first be the great, followed by the greater and then the greatest. It suggests that there is a specific order in which they occur and we must take notice of it if they will be beneficial.

The Order

Love's placement is the only one clearly stated in our opening scripture as the greatest. For the orderly arrangement of the remaining two, faith and hope, we look elsewhere in scripture.

> *"Now faith is the substance of things hoped for, the evidence of things not seen" (Hebrews 11:1; NKJV).*

From the above passage, whatever a person hopes for, faith is its substance. Implying that, hope must exist in order for faith to be its substance. Therefore, hope comes before faith.

Thus, the right order in which they occur is hope, faith and love. We can then state that hope is the great, faith is the greater, and love is the greatest.

TEST YOUR UNDERSTANDING OF CHAPTER 1

1. How many virtues are listed in 1 Corinthians 13:13?

2. List the virtues in any order of preference.

3. What is the original order of the virtues listed in 1 Corinthians 13:13?

4. Still in 1 Corinthians 13:13, show which virtue is repeated in the passage.

5. What is the degree of grammatical comparison used for the virtue mentioned twice?

6. From the same passage, can you detect the clue that suggests the specific order in which the virtues are arranged?

7. Which other biblical text reveals the order of occurrence of the virtues?

8. How many virtues are listed in that passage?

9. What should be the proper biblical order of all the virtues?

10. What new thing have you learned from this chapter?

CHAPTER 2

What Is Hope?

"What the righteous hope for will end in joy; what the wicked expect will come to nothing" (Proverbs 10:28; CJB).

In the previous chapter, we concluded that hope is the great virtue, the first among the three. My simplified definition is that, *"Hope is a joyful and confident expectation of a desired good based on what God has promised."* In other words, to desire something good, accompanied with an expectation or a belief of obtaining it is hope. Two key words emerge in the definition. These are "desire" and "expectation."

Desire

Desire is a strong feeling of wanting to have or possess something or wishing for something to happen or materialize. It may be a longing for what is not attainable, or for what is attainable but not within reach at that moment. That feeling or longing is an expression of the soul, specifically, an emotional state or reaction.

A person must desire what is good and that good must be attainable for it to be dependable. If not, there is the potential to destroy the one who longs for it. In addition, if a desire is not attainable, it can cause hopelessness, which may lead to depression and eventually result in the loss of life, such as suicide.

> *"When hope is crushed, the heart is crushed, but a wish come true fills you with joy" (Proverbs 13:12; GNB).*

Nevertheless, once attainable, it is all right if a desire is not within reach, because the other virtues must be set in motion for it to materialize. We shall discover this in the course of our study.

Expectation

Expectation is the anticipation of something happening, that is, a confident belief or strong hope that a particular event will happen. Its posture is to wait for, look forward to, or look out for something to happen or arrive. It is to anticipate the fulfillment of a desire.

Expectation is an exercise of the soul, precisely, a mental perception of things that are yet to come.

Joy is a character of love, an ingredient of the fruit of the Spirit (Galatians 5:22). The Spirit of joy is significant to hope because it produces the strength of conviction to eliminate all doubt. It also makes time irrelevant because it is a suitable spiritual virtue for every situation.

Joy sustains a person's interest. In fact, Jacob's hope of marrying Rachel derived its strength from the spirit of joy. The joy of love that he had was so intense that it meant nothing when he served for seven years as Rachel's dowry.

Scripture states, *"So Jacob served seven years for Rachel, and they seemed only a few days to him because of the love he had for her." (Genesis 29:20, NKJV).* Despite all the years of hard labor he endured, Laban gave him Leah, Rachel's elder sister instead. He had to have her "on credit" and later pay another dowry for seven more years.

Confidence is the belief or trust in somebody or something, or in the ability of somebody or something to act in a proper, trustworthy, or reliable manner. That implies confidence is faith. It is therefore no surprise that the term *belief* or *trust* is included in the definition of hope.

Therefore, once a desire is attainable, joy and confidence are produced for hope to be sustained until its fulfillment [Hope = Desire + Expectation or Confident Belief].

TEST YOUR UNDERSTANDING OF CHAPTER 2

1. What is the author's definition of hope?

2. Which words emerge from this definition?

3. Which part of the soul experiences and expresses desire?

4. Which part of the soul experiences and expresses expectation?

5. When is a desire dependable?

6. Is it possible for a desire to be good and attainable but not yet within reach?

7. What should a person do with a good and attainable desire that is not yet within his or her reach?

8. How is the Spirit of joy significant to hope?

9. What role do joy and confidence play in attaining a desire?

10. Write the simple formula for hope.

CHAPTER 3

The Purpose of Hope

"19 We have this hope as an anchor for the soul, firm and secure. It enters the inner sanctuary behind the curtain, 20 where Jesus, who went before us, has entered on our behalf" (Hebrews 6:19-20; NIV).

In the previous chapter, we learned that both instances of hope, namely, desire and expectation, apply to the soul. While "desire" emanates from the emotion, the mind engages in "expectation".

Purpose is defined as the reason for which something exists or for which it is made or has been done. There is a definite reason for the existence of hope. We realize this from the above passage. Hope is depicted as an anchor for the soul.

An Anchor for the Soul

Due to the waves caused by the wind, a ship can drift away and be lost at sea. An anchor is a heavy object, typically having a metal shank with a pair of curved, barbed flukes used to moor a ship to the sea bottom. It helps to keep it afloat and hold it in place.

The ancient anchors were much like the modern ones with iron hooks to grapple the rocks and so hold on to prevent shipwreck.

The bible describes the soul as a ship on the sea caught in a constant battle against the waves of the wind of false doctrines and wrong information. Such onslaughts incite fleshly lusts or inordinate affections to bombard the soul with insecurity and instability.

> *"Beloved, I beg you as sojourners and pilgrims, abstain from fleshly lusts which war against the soul" (1 Peter 2:11; NKJV).*

As strangers in this world, there is the tendency that someone may succumb to the incessant attacks and lose his soul. In order to remain stable, it requires the anchor of a trustworthy promise.

No wonder the scripture refers to hope as the anchor of the soul, something that gives it security and stability. Indeed, it is an indispensable device for our faith walk.

Desire's Direction and Destination

A person who moves from place to place without a known destination or purpose is known as a wanderer. Such a movement is aimless and hopeless, like a mirage, always on the go but never reaching a destination.

In the same way, a wandering desire may be one that craves for anything good or bad, or right or wrong, without taking into account the resultant effect. The literal meaning of the wandering of the desire is "the walking of the soul."

> *"Better is the sight of the eyes [the enjoyment of what is available to one] than the cravings of wandering desire. This is also vanity (emptiness, falsity, and futility) and a striving after the wind and a feeding on it!" (Ecclesiastes 6:9; AMP).*

God: The Mainstay of the soul

Without hope, it is obvious that the human soul will drift away, like a ship without an anchor, and be lost forever.

"Why are you downcast, O my soul? Why so disturbed within me? Put your hope in God, for I will yet praise him, my Savior and my God" (Psalms 42:11; NIV).

God is life's constant. He does not change. All other things are variables. Without a constant, everything will fall apart. It reminds me of Chinua Achebe's English Literature book entitled, "Things Fall Apart." A caption in it reads, "…the center cannot hold."

God is the anchor of hope, the center that holds life. This anchor of hope is both sure and steadfast. It will not slip or lose its grip. He is a spirit. He is invisible. Yet, without Him, souls will perish like a floating balloon without control or a high-flying kite whose string snaps.

Just as an anchor is out of sight, so also hope goes beyond the veil of the flesh into the inner faculty of the soul. The anchor is out of sight, but it holds firmly and securely, and that is what matters. Similarly, hope is unseen but it serves the twofold purpose of certainty and stability. That is what matters.

TEST YOUR UNDERSTANDING OF CHAPTER 3

1. How is hope depicted in Hebrews 6:19?

2. Though believers in Christ are "Beloved", they are at war. Who is their enemy?

3. Though believers in Christ are "Beloved", why at they are war?

4. Which part of the human faculty is engaged in the war?

5. How does the bible describe the soul and its location in this context of war?

6. What represents the wind that generates the waves to cause instability and insecurity of the soul?

7. What is the purpose of hope?

8. What is required for the soul to remain stable?

9. A reliable promise is the hope that anchors the soul from wandering about. True or False?

10. According to Psalm 42:11, what will cause a soul to be downcast and disturbed?

CHAPTER 4

What Is Faith?

"Now faith is the substance of things hoped for, the evidence of things not seen" *(Hebrews 11:1).*

In chapter one, we concluded that faith is the greater virtue, the second among the three. In defining it as stated in the above text, we need to consider the following points:

1. It is the substance of things hoped for.
2. It is the evidence of things not seen.

Two main words that stand out are *substance* and *evidence*, and the corresponding phrases are "hoped for" and "not seen" respectively.

Substance = Title Deed

The first word that is translated s*ubstance* comes from the Greek word *hupostasis* and derived from *huphistêmi* – a compound of *hupo*, which means "under," and *histêmi*, which refers to what stands under anything such as a building, a contract, or a promise.

This word means *a support, groundwork, confidence.* It represents the thing that stands as a support under another; for instance, a chair, a foundation, a pillar or the root of a tree. Similarly, official or legal documents such as title deeds or contracts serve as the basis for trust between agreeing parties. That is to say, a title deed is the substance.

A married couple lived in a house they owned. Unknown to them, the title deed covering the property got missing shortly before the husband passed away. They found out only when they needed it. After the demise of the man, it became the widow's onerous responsibility to retrieve the document.

What baffles me is the concern over papers when she already lives in the house. Nevertheless, her agitation is justified because an owner may transfer his property to a beneficiary but only the legal document gives vesting assent or entitlement to the beneficiary. That is to say, the title vests the property in the beneficiary.

In the definition, a clear relationship between hope and faith is established where faith is the substance of things hoped for. It implies that whenever a person desires something, faith is the title deed that converts a beneficiary's expectation into his actual possession of the real thing.

Evidence = Conviction + Persuasion

The second word translated *evidence* comes from the Greek word *elegchos* which means "proof", "conviction", "reproof" or "certain persuasion." This word denotes what gives a sign or proof of the existence or truth of something, or helps somebody to come to a particular conclusion.

Traditionally, *to convince* somebody is to make him or her certain or sure, having complete confidence in the truth of something or an expected outcome. *To persuade* somebody is to convince him or her to act. Consequently, the phrase "certain persuasion" implies fully convincing a person to act in line with that conviction.

Thus, faith is the moral conviction of the truth of anything, or the foundation or basis for belief and corresponding action. In other words, faith serves as the basis for belief and action [Faith = Belief + Action].

The Evidence of Creation

The context of Hebrews 11:1 is about the universe coming into existence. Besides, the scripture states emphatically in verse three: *"Faith convinces us that God created the world through his word. This means what can be seen was made by something that could not be seen" (GW).* No one can claim to have witnessed creation because the human race was not in existence at the time. How then can one testify of something he has not witnessed?

God did not create the world out of nothing. He created it by His Word; the invisible created the visible. There are seen things and unseen things or there are visible things and invisible things. The activity of creation occurred in eternity within the invisible or unseen realm. Therefore, each person needs faith to be convinced about creation and the unseen Person – the Creator – behind it.

Conviction in the Heart

A woman had suffered from severe bleeding for twelve years without any medical solution. Rather than improve, her condition continued to deteriorate with time. According to Mark's gospel account, she heard about Jesus one day and decided to touch the edge of His robe for her bleeding to stop.

Since there is no medical procedure that stops hemorrhaging that way, one may ask how she came by the idea. We find the answer in Matthew 9:21; *"For she said within herself, If I may but touch his garment, I shall be whole."* The expression *"she said within herself"* is indicative of the voice of her inner man also known as her spirit or her heart.

Different versions put the same phrase differently— "she thought", "she said to herself", "she had been saying to herself", "she was thinking." Each version brings out a unique aspect of meditation, which involves thinking, whispering and proclaiming aloud.

1. She naturally heard about Jesus.
    *   That information gave her hope.
    *   We have the same experience reading the bible, mental knowledge.

2. She began to think about what she heard naturally.
   - That exercise is meditation.
   - We can also think about or meditate on the scriptures.

3. She said to herself or her inner spirit spoke to her soul.
   - That is *rhema* – same as the spoken or revealed word of God.
   - Faith comes by hearing in our spirits.
   - Our spirits hear by the *rhema* or spoken word of God, not the written word.

4. The message her spirit uttered was "If only I may touch His garment, I shall be made well."
   - Her spirit knew what to do.
   - That is the same as believing, understanding, or having faith.
   - However, she needed the cooperation of her soul to know what to do, and the involvement of her body by acting according to that specific *rhema*.

5. Her persuasion moved her to act despite the many possible obstacles.
   - Faith without works is dead faith.

- She put her faith in action.

The message required her to act because the Word of the Lord told her spirit "if only." It means she had no option. Her spirit told her physical senses what to do. She eventually did it. She moved physically and touched Jesus physically.

At the same time, her spirit also touched Jesus spiritually. How do we know this? It was her spirit who said "If only I…" Her human spirit wanted an avenue to touch the hem of Jesus' robe. She worked at it and that was how her twelve years of bleeding became history.

Christ the Word

Faith is the official document that gives a firm assurance of the things expected, and the proof that convinces a person in his heart of things that he does not see – i.e. things invisible to his natural senses.

The Amplified Version of Hebrews 11:1 reads: *"NOW FAITH is the assurance (the confirmation, the title deed) of the things [we] hope for, being the proof of things [we] do not see and the conviction of their reality [faith perceiving as real fact what is not revealed to the senses]."* Simply put, faith is hope's legal papers, which cause the heart to be convinced about the unseen.

God, in the Person of Jesus Christ, is the evidence that manifests in view of the substance of His word to uphold all things (Hebrews 1:3). Thus, from the beginning of what we hope for through to the end where we see the manifestation, Christ is the object of our faith (Hebrews 3:14, 11:6; Romans 8:32; ISV). [Substance = the Word (logos), Evidence = the living and active word (rhema)].

TEST YOUR UNDERSTANDING OF CHAPTER 4

1. What is faith?

2. Identify the two main words that stand out in the definition of faith and write their corresponding phrases by them.

3. The substance of faith is the same as title deed or contract. True or False?

4. What does the phrase "certain persuasion" imply?

5. Give a brief formula of faith.

6. God created the world out of nothing. True or False?

7. What does it take a person to be convinced about creation and the unseen Creator?

8. How many times did the woman with the issue of blood hear about Jesus?

9. How did she hear on each occasion?

10. How did she position herself to hear each time?

CHAPTER 5

Divine Authority

"But as many as received Him, to them He gave the right to become children of God, to those who believe in His name" (John 1:12; NKJV).

In the previous chapter, we learnt that the legal aspect of faith is the scripture or the written word. The viewing aspect that gives you conviction in your heart that the written document is genuine is the understanding or revelation you receive from God through His Word concerning the matter.

The Author of Creation

The word *authority* comes from the root word *author*. The primary sense is one who brings forth something or causes a thing to come forth. Expressions such as *originator, creator, father, initiator or beginner,* all refer to the one who brings something into existence.

Several passages such as John 1:1-3 and Ephesians 3:9 ascribe proprietorship or ownership of all things to God. He founded the heavens and the earth and everything in them. He is the fabricator, the manufacturer.

The Divine "Power of Attorney"

He created all things by His Word. It is important to recognize the Word as a Person who is Himself God (Revelations. 19:13). The Word of God and the Name Jesus Christ refer to the same Person. He possesses the highest authority in the entire universe.

God fully grants all promises in Christ backed by all the honor of His Name (Psalms 138:2; NLT). Therefore, His promises written in the bible are the same as the title deed. They represent the highest authority in Christ that one can ever attain.

Delegation

One Greek word for authority is *exousia*. It has various meanings. The one related to our study is *conferred power, delegated empowerment or authorization, operating in a designated jurisdiction.* Each of the words "conferred", "delegated", or "designated" suggests a gift or a privilege from one person to another.

Delegated power refers to the authority God gives to His saints – authorizing them to act to the extent that He guides them by faith in His word. He has chosen us to represent Him, being empowered to act, make decisions, or allocate resources on His behalf. He has formally appointed us to his position and duty. From His word, we derive and exercise His title, honor, and favor.

Substance or Title Deed is Authority

The substance of faith, the title deed, the written Word, is our authority from God. It is our power of attorney. It empowers us to act on God's behalf in spiritual and legal business matters.

Once we believe with our hearts what is written concerning us in Christ, we possess the right to access and enjoy the privileges enumerated in the scriptures; for "…with the heart man believes unto righteousness…" (Romans 10:10). Man is right when he believes God's Word.

Authority in this context therefore, is the permit from the author or owner to another person he has sent to represent him, specifically to manifest, display or exhibit His nature, character or abilities. Every believer in Christ possesses delegated authority and power to act as His ambassador on earth.

TEST YOUR UNDERSTANDING OF CHAPTER 5

1. What is the legal aspect of biblical faith?

2. What is the viewing aspect that gives you conviction in your heart?

3. What is the root word for authority?

4. Who is the author of creation?

5. By what did the author create everything?

6. The Word of God and the Name Jesus Christ refer to the same Person. True or False?

7. Who possesses the highest authority in the entire universe?

8. What is the Greek word for authority mentioned in the chapter?

9. Who can exercise God's divine power of attorney and why?

10. What is expected of the people God has chosen to represent Him?

CHAPTER 6

…And Divine Power

"18 I pray also that the eyes of your heart may be enlightened in order that you may know…19… his incomparably great power for us who believe. That power is like the working of his mighty strength, 20 which he exerted in Christ when he raised him from the dead and seated him at his right hand in the heavenly realms" (Ephesians 1:18-20; NIV).

Power is the ability, strength, and capacity to do something. From the definition, we find three terms – ability, strength, and capacity.

1. Power is ability: being able or well equipped to handle circumstances and extents, and well positioned to handle the timing – knowing the best moment, when to act.

2. Power is strength: that is the physical condition needed to exert considerable force, e.g. in lifting, pulling, or pushing something.

3. Power is capacity: that is something big enough or has enough size to accommodate and accomplish a task.

Dunamis

One of the four Greek words used in the above passage to reveal the power of Christ is "dunamis." It means inherent power or power residing in a thing by virtue of its nature. The New International Version states that the power is incomparably great. It is unequaled in quality, excellent, outstanding, or unique as to have no equal. It is also great in magnitude, extremely more than usual.

Dynamic Power

From "dunamis" comes the English word "dynamite" – a class of explosives used in mining or blasting. God's power is explosive like dynamite. It is dynamic in its working. When active in motion, it produces change and development consistent with the change and development it undergoes.

The Believer's Power

The dynamic power that causes changes is for those who believe, and those who believe are the ones who understand the scriptures. When a person knows the scriptures mentally, he cannot experience its inherent power until he meditates on it and gets the true meaning. That brings conviction. Like the seed of a potential tree, its life remains dormant until it is sown. Once sown, the power within is activated and life unfolds [Belief = Knowledge + Conviction].

Evidence or Inner Conviction is Power

Evidence or inner conviction unpacks the power in the Word, namely, its nature, character and ability, and makes it ready to act with unparalleled force. This explains the inherent power or power residing in a thing by virtue of its nature.

Authority always goes with power. Without power of enforcement, authority is vain, or mere, empty words. On the other hand, power is illegitimate without authority or granting of legal, official permission.

TEST YOUR UNDERSTANDING OF CHAPTER 6

1. What is power?

2. What is the Greek word used for power in the chapter?

3. Which English word originates from "dunamis"?

4. What does the English word represent?

5. God's power is explosive and dynamic in its working. True or False?

6. Describe God's power when active in motion.

7. Who are those who believe?

8. What is the nature of a believer's power?

9. Why is it that a person can know the scriptures mentally but cannot experience the power of the word?

10. How can a person experience the power of God's word?

CHAPTER 7

The Positions of
Hope and Faith in Man

*"But since we belong to the day, let us be
self-controlled, putting on faith and love as
a breastplate, and the hope of salvation as a
helmet" (1 Thessalonians 5:8; NIV).*

Once again, we find the three extremely important
virtues listed together in the above scripture. This
time it is not about the order of their occurrence. Rather,
the verse indicates their positions in a person.

The bible identifies faith and love as breastplates
and hope as a helmet. A breastplate is a piece of armor
that covers the chest, which is the region of the heart. A

helmet is a hard protective piece of armor used for covering the head.

Spiritual Armors

It is interesting to note that hope, faith and love are devices. It is even more interesting that they are parts of a Christian soldier's armor worn for protection in spiritual battles. The mind requires the first device, hope. The heart requires the last two devices, faith and love.

Hope is in the Mind

The head is the region of the mind. Thus, *hope* is set in the region of the *mind*. It is a mental attitude of expectancy concerning the future.

Faith is in the Heart

Faith is located in the region of the *heart*. It is a condition of the heart, producing something so real within us here and now that the word *substance* can fit its description.

The Point of Entry

"For the word of God is living and powerful, and sharper than any two-edged sword, piercing even to the division of soul and spirit, and of joints and marrow, and is a discerner of the thoughts and intents of the heart" (Hebrews 4:12; NKJV).

The above passage reveals a peculiar order. The soul comes first, followed by the spirit, and then the joints and marrows. The soul here is in reference to the mind or the intellect, which deals with knowledge.

The spirit is the heart, the inward man. Joints and marrows denote the body – flesh and blood. Thus, God's Word first enters the mind, and then, into the heart. Once in the heart, it can affect the body when proclaimed consistently. This is the route of God's Word in a man's life.

TEST YOUR UNDERSTANDING OF CHAPTER 7

1. What does the passage in 1 Thessalonians 5:8 indicate about the virtues?

2. What is a helmet?

3. What does a helmet represent in the passage?

4. What is a breastplate?

5. What does it represent in the passage?

6. Can you identify the point of entry of God's word in a man's life?

7. Can you identify the second route of God's word in a man's life?

8. Can you identify the third route of God's word in a man's life?

9. How many of the virtues are needed in the mind?

10. How many of the virtues are needed in the heart?

CHAPTER 8

Understanding Faith and Belief

"It is written: "I believed; therefore I have spoken"" (2 Corinthians 4:13; NIV).

Faith and belief are not the same. However, some people wrongly use them interchangeably. So, exactly what does it mean to believe?

Belief is the acceptance by the mind that something is true or real, reinforced by a spiritual sense of certainty in the heart. Thus, belief begins with the mental acceptance of written facts and then held as truth after a firm conviction in the heart.

Faith = Belief + Action

Belief is part of faith but faith is more than belief. Faith comprises belief and the corresponding action in line with what we believe. Faith has a 'principle' part and a 'practical' part. The 'principle' or written part is a fundamental truth or proposition serving as the foundation for belief or action. The 'practical' part is the part concerned with action – the actual application or use of a plan or method, as opposed to the theories relating to it.

Apart from the written aspect of faith, which a person must believe through the knowledge and understanding of the scriptures, there is the part that requires continuous action. Faith must be expressed in a practical way based on the written facts and revealed truth of the scriptures with positive effect on character and life.

Below is a summary of the combination of the scriptures and the Person and work of Christ, and its effect on character and life:

1. Belief:
   - Faith meditates on or thinks deeply about the facts of the scriptures.

- Faith believes in the revealed truth based on the scriptures by forming mental pictures of the words of the bible.

  Believing what "...is written" (John 20:31).

2. Passion or love:
   - Faith leads to the affectionate belief in the Person of Christ.
   - Faith leads to the affectionate belief in the work of Christ.

   All the scriptures – "It is written" – attest to Him (John 5:39).

3. Total Commitment:
   - Faith is the confidence in the absolute authority of Christ.
   - Faith is the constant rest in the absolute power of Christ.

   Commit to Him once; keep trusting Him every day (Psalms 37:5).

4. Persistent Action:
   - Faith is the mental impression or perception of the facts of the scriptures.

- Faith is the practical affirmation in line with the revealed truth of the scriptures.

Your faith is activated when you confess what you believe, and it remains active when you keep confessing what you believe ......"Therefore have I spoken" (2 Corinthians 4:13).

TEST YOUR UNDERSTANDING OF CHAPTER 8

1. Faith and belief are the same. True or False?

2. Where does belief begin and where does it end?

3. Where does belief end?

4. How many parts has faith?

5. Name the parts of faith.

6. State the formula that proves the relationship between faith and belief.

7. Which part of faith requires a person to believe through the knowledge and understanding of the scriptures?

8. Which part of faith requires continuous action for its expression?

9. What should and person believe and how?

10. Who should be the absolute and reliable object of man's faith?

CHAPTER 9

The Similarities
Between Hope and Faith

Now, let us look at the qualities that hope and faith have in common.

1. **Attitude:**

   An attitude is a personal view, that is, an opinion or general feeling about something.

   - Hope is an attitude of certainty.
   - Faith is an attitude of certainty.

   Scriptures:

"But the Messiah, as Son, was faithful over God's house. And we are that house of his, provided we hold firmly to the courage and confidence inspired by what we hope for" (Hebrews 3:6; CJB).

"1 Now faith is being sure of what we hope for and certain of what we do not see. 2 This is what the ancients were commended for" (Hebrews 11:1-2; NIV).

Christians of all times – both Jew and Gentile – constitute God's spiritual house. Individually, our bodies are the temples of the Holy Spirit. Collectively, we are the temple of the living God. For us to achieve His elective purpose, we do not have to lose hope. We do not have to waver in doubt. We do not have to hesitate or hold back. Hope in the mind inspires confidence because there is an imminent expectation. Faith in the heart generates joy and gladness because of the conviction of fulfillment. We must be bold, firm, and consistent in declaring what we hope for to the end as if we already possess it. This is the way to prove that we are God's house and that He lives in us. The phrase, "...hope till the end..." further proves that hope remains throughout.

2. Dependability:

A thing is dependable when others need it for their existence or survival. It is something to trust in, rest on, rely on, or lean on because one has complete confidence in it.

- Belief is part of hope and that is what makes it dependable.
- Belief is part of faith and that is what makes it dependable.

Scripture:
"You will keep him in perfect peace, Whose mind is stayed on You, Because he trusts in You" (Isaiah 26:3; NKJV).

The human mind and heart are burden bearers. The mind bears the mental, intellectual and emotional burdens. The heart bears the spiritual burdens. However, they are both not self-sufficient in themselves because they are not self-existent. God is self-existent and self-sufficient. He created all things though He does not need anything. All creatures depend on Him for existence and upkeep. His unchanging nature, character of faithfulness, and omnipotent ability are the basis for trusting Him. A mind focused on God has hope. A heart that trusts in God has faith. Such combination guarantees assurance or perfect peace. Perfect peace is actually *shalom shalom*–peace, peace–or double peace. One peace is in the mind. The other peace is in the heart. God's kind of peace is beyond every reasonable doubt – Philippians 4:7-9.

3. **Existence:**

The word is defined as the state of being real, actual, or current, rather than imagined, invented, or obsolete.

- Hope is a reality. It is actual and current.
- Faith is also a reality. It is actual and current.

Scripture:

"Faith means being sure of the things we hope for and knowing that something is real even if we do not see it" (Hebrews 11:1; NCV).

A substance is matter, having mass and occupying space. This definition comes from the point of view that everything must be physical in order to be tangible. However, the human senses relate to the immediate environment. The natural senses relate to the natural setting and the spiritual senses perceive the spiritual realm. Hope and faith are both spiritual realities and function from the spiritual realm. That is why the physical senses cannot perceive them. Hope is real but unseen, faith is also real but unseen. It takes faith to be sure of hope. It takes the same faith to experience reality even if we do not see it.

4. **Nature:**
Nature is the basic features, qualities, or character of a person. His inborn characteristics determine his personality.

- The nature of hope is spiritual, not physical.
- The nature of faith is spiritual, not physical.

Scripture:
"In hope of eternal life, which God, that cannot lie, promised before the world began" (Titus 1:2).

"It is written: "I believed; therefore I have spoken." With that same spirit of faith we also believe and therefore speak" (2 Corinthians 4:13; NIV).

God promised the hope of eternal life before the world began. That is an eternal promise made by an eternal and self-existing God who does not change and cannot lie. That makes hope a spiritual virtue, not physical. In the same way, the scripture attests to faith as a spiritual virtue. It demonstrates how the spirit of faith works, that is, by believing the written word and continuously speaking it aloud.

5. **Realm:**

A realm is the atmosphere that dominates a region and all that it contains. The region may have well-defined boundaries. However, its atmosphere may traverse its scope.

- Hope operates in the unseen realm but can influence the seen realm too.
- Faith also operates in the unseen realm but can influence the seen realm too.

Scriptures:
"24 For we were saved in this hope, but hope that is seen is not hope; for why does one still hope for what he sees? 25 But if we hope for what we do not see, we eagerly wait for it with perseverance" (Romans 8:24-25; NKJV).

"Now faith is the...evidence of things not seen" (Hebrews 11:1; NKJV)

There is a realm – the physical realm – that is visible to the natural eye. Only through the faculty of sight does it have knowledge and apparent qualities of existence. There is another realm – the spiritual realm – that is invisible to the natural eye. The spiritual realm is not limited to the three dimensions of length, breadth and height like our physical world. For instance, instead of seeing life from the perspective of unseen realities, Adam and Eve were spiritually blinded to the invisible realm of God. They rather focused on the three-dimensional world to their own detriment and that of the entire human race (Genesis 3:7).

6. Duration:

Duration is the period of time that something exists or lasts.

- Hope is eternal.
- Faith is eternal.

Scriptures:
"And now abide faith, hope, love, these three…" (1 Corinthians 13:13; NKJV).

"while we do not look at the things which are seen, but at the things which are not seen. For the things which are seen are temporary, but the things which are not

seen are eternal" (2 Corinthians 4:18; NKJV).

There are things that are seen and things that are unseen. Seen things are temporary while unseen things are eternal. Hope and faith are eternal, having no beginning or end. Hope conceives a desire in the mind. The heart receives what hope conceives by believing. Faith acts out what the heart believes. Then the one who acts experiences the manifestation.

7. **Settlement:**
It is the payment of a bill, debt, or claim.

- Hope is a promise in Christ.
- Faith is a promise in Christ.

Scripture:
"So when Jesus had received the sour wine, He said, "It is finished!" And bowing His head, He gave up His spirit" (John 19:30; NKJV).

When Jesus said, "It is finished", every price for man's sin was paid with His blood. On that basis, the Lord forgives all iniquities, heals all diseases, and delivers from destruction. He crowns with lovingkindness and tender mercies and renews the life of the beneficiary like that of the eagle by completely filling him with good things (Psalms 103:3-5).

8. Affirmation:

It is an assertion of support or agreement. God has surely granted all His promises in Christ.

- Hope is a guaranteed promise in Christ.
- Faith is a guaranteed promise in Christ.

Scripture:
"For all the promises of God in Him are Yes, and in Him Amen, to the glory of God through us" (2 Corinthians 1:20; NKJV).

"Yes" is an adverb used, especially in speech, to indicate assent, agreement, or affirmation God never made empty promises. He gave the Holy Spirit to all believers as a security to confirm His promise. Moreover, He grants authority and power to anyone who believes in Jesus as Lord.

9. **Offer:**

To offer is to provide, furnish, make available or accessible. God's promises are open checks to all who belong to Christ.

- Hope is an expectation already given in Christ.
- Faith is an expectation already given in Christ.

Scripture:
"22 whether Paul or Apollos or Peter, or the world, or life and death, or the present and the future. Everything belongs to you, 23 and you belong to Christ, and Christ belongs to God" (1 Corinthians 3:22, 23; NLT).

Scripture makes it clear that Christ owns all that belongs to God. These include human beings, the world, life and death, the present and the future. All belong to Him. Every promise of God is fulfilled in

Him. Therefore, once you belong to Him, all things are yours. This is a clear confirmation that we are heirs of God and joint-heirs with Christ.

10. Acceptance:

Acceptance is the willing receipt of a gift or payment.

- Hope is an expectation accessed only in Christ.
- Faith is an expectation accessed only in Christ.

Scripture:
"2 Beloved, now we are children of God; and it has not yet been revealed what we shall be, but we know that when He is revealed, we shall be like Him, for we shall see Him as He is. 3 And everyone who has this hope in Him purifies himself, just as He is pure" (1 John 3:2, 3; NKJV).

Even though hope precedes faith in order of degrees, one needs faith to take control of hope–the future–now. "What we shall be" is hope. However, that depends on who we are now – faith. We are God's children by faith in Jesus Christ. Only those who confess Jesus as Lord can access God's promises.

TEST YOUR UNDERSTANDING OF CHAPTER 9

1. How many similarities between hope and faith are listed in the chapter?

2. What does hope in the mind inspire and why?

3. What does faith in the heart generate?

4. How do we prove that we are God's house and that He lives in us?

5. What makes hope and faith dependable?

6. The human mind and heart are burden bearers. Which burdens does the mind bear? Which burden does the heart bear?

7. Hope is real but unseen, faith is also real but unseen. True or False?

8. Seen things are temporary while unseen things are eternal. Where do you place hope and faith?

9. What is a clear confirmation that we are heirs of God and joint-heirs with Christ?

10. Note down your personal benefit (s) from reading this chapter.

CHAPTER 10

The Differences
Between Hope and Faith

Hope and faith differ in four main aspects. These differences together serve as the key to understanding the subject.

1. **Position:**

    Position is the suitable place where something is located or put.

    - Hope is located in the mind–mental.
    - Faith is located in the heart–spiritual.

    Scripture:

"But let us who are of the day be sober, putting on the breastplate of faith and love, and as a helmet the hope of salvation" (1 Thessalonians 5:8; NKJV).

Hope is a mental attitude guided by the information received through our physical senses. Faith is a spiritual condition of the heart based on the mental attitude of hope. A godly desire in the mind is hope. A godly desire in the heart is faith. As food in the mouth is swallowed into the stomach to benefit the body, so also the same desire in the mind must be believed in the heart to cause a miraculous effect.

2. **Period:**

It is an interval or portion of time; the moment that something lasts or exists.

- Hope is a period directed toward the unspecified future.
- Faith is the same hope considered as established now.

Scripture:

59

"1 We have been made right with God because of our faith. So we have peace with God through our Lord Jesus Christ. 2 Through our faith, Christ has brought us into that blessing of God's grace that we now enjoy. And we are very happy because of the hope we have of sharing God's glory" (Romans 5:1, 2; ERV).

The future is a moment that is yet to come. The present is the moment when something is currently happening, taking place or existing. If hope is not locked down with faith, expectations will be cut off, disappointed or never be fulfilled.

3. Prospect:
Prospect is the possibility of the occurrence of something desirable that is capable of existing, happening or being achieved.

- Hope has the possibility of occurrence.
- Faith is actual occurrence.

Scripture:

"...the bridegroom came. Then those who were ready went in with him to the marriage feast, and the door was locked. 11 Later, when the other five bridesmaids returned, they stood outside, calling, 'Lord! Lord! Open the door for us!' 12 "But he called back, 'Believe me, I don't know you!' 13 "So you, too, must keep watch! For you do not know the day or hour of my return" (Matthew 25:10-13; NLT).

Hope is a potential, having the prospect or the possibility of occurrence. Its latent qualities or abilities have the capacity to develop, succeed, or become something beneficial in the future. However, because hope is not confined to a specified period, its usefulness remains a probability. On the other hand, the definite moment of faith is "now." Hence, faith is the actual occurrence of a desire. Faith deliberately changes the period of hope from the future tense to the present or even the past tense. Faith lays hold on the promise as if it has been fulfilled already and considers it actually done. The mistake of the five foolish virgins was that they anticipated the coming of the bridegroom. Yet, because he did not specify his time of arrival, they were not ready. They were not fully prepared for immediate action. Hope alone will definitely disappoint, but hope converted to faith will never disappoint.

4. Perception:

It is the process of acquiring information about the surrounding environment or situation through the senses.

- Hope is an already received expectation that is yet to be experienced.
- Faith is the already received expectation of hope being experienced now.

Scripture:
"When there was nothing left to hope for, Abraham still hoped and believed. As a result, he became a father of many nations, as he had been told: "That is how many descendants you will have" (Romans 4:18; GW).

From the above passage, we discover that Abraham had both hope and faith – hope concerning the future and faith for the present. No matter the hopelessness of a situation, we must be mindful of what we hope for and what we have received now to lock down that hope in the present. God's promise is the absolute basis for hope, which He guarantees anyone who believes in His written Word.

TEST YOUR UNDERSTANDING OF CHAPTER 10

1. In how many aspects do hope and faith differ? List them in order.

2. Show the difference between hope and faith with respect to the first aspect.

3. Show the difference between hope and faith with respect to the second aspect.

4. Show the difference between hope and faith with respect to the third aspect.

5. A godly desire in the heart is hope. True or False?

6. A godly desire in the mind is faith. True or False?

7. Faith is a spiritual condition of the heart based on the mental attitude of hope. True or False?

8. State the difference between the future and the present.

9. Why would the expectation of hope remain a probability?

10. What can be done to fulfil the desires hoped for?

CHAPTER 11

How Each Device Works

"17 As it is written: "I have made you a father of many nations." He is our father in the sight of God, in whom he believed — the God who gives life to the dead and calls things that are not as though they were" (Romans 4:17; NIV).

Hope has a language called *the word of hope.* Likewise, faith has a language called *the word of faith.* Because hope and faith differ in time and position, the expressions and tenses used in speech also differ.

1. Statements of Position:

Position is the place where somebody or something is, especially in relation to other things. By now, we know that hope deals with the future while faith deals with the present. It is therefore important for the believer to be conscious of where he or she stands in relation to hope and faith. That will help to determine what to say and what not to say. As we already know, hope is a joyful and confident expectation of a desired good based on what God has promised. The strength of hope is in His faithfulness.

"Let us continue to hold firmly to the hope that we confess without wavering, for the one who made the promise is faithful" *(Hebrews 10:23; ISV).*

Concerning hope, the believer's position in Christ is only for the appearing of our Lord Jesus Christ. This event will culminate in the resurrection of the dead in Christ and the rapture of the saints (1 Thessalonians 4:14-17). On the other hand, faith is the title deed of what we hope for and the inner conviction of what we do not see. The strength of faith is in the faith of God.

"As it is written: "I have made you a father of many nations." He is our father in the sight of God, in whom he believed — the God who gives life to the dead and calls things that are not as though they were" (Romans 4:17;NIV).

God calls those things that are not as though they were. That is known as God's faith. Now, believers in Christ have the God-kind of faith, *"And Jesus, answering, said to them, Have God's faith" (Mark 11:22; BBE).* The believer's position concerning faith is always to exercise the God-kind of faith already possessed in Christ.

2. **Statements of Time:**
    The word of hope uses the following future tense expressions:

    "I hope…"
    "I hope so."
    "I expect…"
    "I wish…"
    "I am hoping for."
    "I hope and pray'"
    "I am believing God for."

"I believe I shall receive."
"It shall be well."
"God will do it."
"God bless you."
"God will bless me."

*"Say to the righteous that it shall be well
with them, for they shall eat the fruit of
their deeds" (Isaiah 3:10; AMP).*

The word of faith uses the following present
tense expressions:

"I believe I have received."
"It is well."
"It is done."
"I call it done."
"There is a lifting up for me."
"By the stripes of Jesus, I believe I have been
healed."
"God has done it."
"I am blessed."
"I am persuaded."
"I am anointed."

*"That is why I tell you, whatever you ask
for in prayer, believe that you have*

received it and it will be yours" (Mark 11:24; ISV).

3. The God of Hope and Faith:

God is the God of hope. Meaning, He is the source of hope and lives by it.

"Now may the God of hope fill you with all joy and peace in believing, that you may abound in hope by the power of the Holy Spirit" (Romans 15:13; NKJV).

God is the God of faith. Meaning, He is the source of our faith from beginning to the end and lives by it.

"And Jesus, answering, said to them, Have God's faith" (Mark 11:22; BBE).

He conceives by hope and manifests by faith. As His children by the new birth, we also have to imitate the hope and faith of God our heavenly Father and live by them because the just lives by faith.

4. Examples of God's Hope and Faith:

Within the space of two verses, in the same speech, God reveals His intent and calls it accomplished.

Hope says,
"...**you shall be** a father..."

"As for Me, behold, My covenant is with you, and you shall be a father of many nations" (Genesis 17:4; NKJV).

Faith says,
"...**I have made you** a father..." which is similar to "**you are** a father..."

"No longer shall your name be called Abram, but your name shall be Abraham; for I have made you a father of many nations" (Genesis 17:5; NKJV).

Prophet Isaiah: "We Are Healed"–Isaiah 53:5

At the time of the prophet Isaiah, Christ had not yet paid the price for supernatural healing even though it was an eternal reality in God's mind.

As a prophet who had a revelation of the mind of God, Isaiah spoke from the eternal and spiritual points of view. He did not use the future tense because he did not approach the matter from a physical perspective. That is why he used "ARE" which is the present indicative of the verb "to be."

Apostle Peter: "You Were Healed"–1 Peter 2:24

On the other hand, Peter had the benefit of the historical fulfillment of what Isaiah spoke about, even the same eternal, spiritual reality in God's mind.

Hence, speaking from both viewpoints, he used the past tense "WERE" because he knew that the Lord had already paid on the cross at Calvary. Calvary was post-Isaiah.

God's Word: Far or Near?

"6 But the righteousness of faith speaks in this way, "Do not say in your heart, 'Who will ascend into heaven?'" (that is, to bring Christ down from above) 7 or, "'Who will descend into the abyss?'" (that is, to bring Christ up from the dead). 8 But what does it say? "The word is near you, in your mouth and in your heart" (that is, the word of faith which we preach): 9 that

if you confess with your mouth the Lord Jesus and believe in your heart that God has raised Him from the dead, you will be saved. 10 For with the heart one believes unto righteousness, and with the mouth confession is made unto salvation" (Romans 10:6-10; NKJV).

One very important question you must ask yourself is this: "How near is God's Word to you or how far is it from you? How is it related to you?

In the above passage, we are warned not to imagine in our hearts that Christ must be brought down from heaven above. We should also not think that He is down in the abyss among the dead.

If you appreciate that Christ is the Word of God then you must clearly understand the following:

1. The Word is near you.

2. The Word must be in your heart because with the heart man believes.

3. You must always keep confessing with your mouth the Word that you believe in your heart, to experience it.

TEST YOUR UNDERSTANDING OF CHAPTER 11

1. What is the language of faith called?

2. What is the language of hope called?

3. What is the strength of hope?

4. What is the strength of faith?

5. What is the believer's position concerning hope?

6. What does the believer expect with the appearing of our Lord Jesus Christ?

7. What is God's faith?

8. What is the believer's position concerning faith?

9. Will you classify the expression "God will do it" as the language of hope or faith?

10. When God tells you, "...you shall be a father/mother..." and "...I have made you a father/mother..." which will you consider as the language of faith or hope?

CHAPTER 12

Combining Hope with Faith

"So I tell you this. When you pray to ask God for anything, believe. Believe that you have received that thing. If you do, you will have it" (Mark 11:24; EasyEnglish).

We have already looked at faith as a substance of the thing we expect. That faith must be between hope and the thing we expect in order to bring the desire to fruition. Now let us see how hope and faith function together. Once again, let us recall that faith is the substance or title deed of that thing you desire or want.

The Example of Money

To illustrate the point, let us use the example of money. Assuming you need some money you do not yet have. That desire is in hope. Now, someone gives you a check of a certain amount in response to your need for money. The check becomes the document, assurance, substance, or title deed to the money.

The Check is the Substance

As you have the check, you have the substance of the money you were hoping for. The check is as good as the money in the bank because it is the document that gives you ownership of the money. Moreover, it can be used to transact any business.

The check is seen as cash. Indeed, in commercial transactions, the check is a negotiable instrument and may be transferred from one person to the other for the payment of goods and services. There must be faith (substance, deed, or document) which becomes the basis of possession or ownership.

Three Ways of Ownership

Listed below are three ways by which a person can own a thing:

1. Buy it.

   Buying is an exchange of one thing of value for another through a medium. That medium may be legal tender. Legal tender represents the document or title deed. The State has a legal tender, and if anyone is in possession of it, he has the right to exchange it for something of equal value.

2. Inherit it.

   The second way of owning a thing is by inheritance, usually done through a Will. Inheritance, properly so-called is effective upon the death of the testator or owner of the estate. The Will must come into effect to validate one's right to inherit.

3. Receive it as a gift.

   The third means of ownership is by receiving as a gift a thing given willingly to someone without payment. It is the free transfer of possession of a present, causing another to receive or have.

   Therefore, to become an owner is not something that just happens. All forms of ownership have legal implications and require documentation. [Substance = title deed = authority of the owner].

Verification

Beyond the document part, there is the viewing part. The evidential value of the desire or thing in question is determined by verifying that indeed it exists, thus, verifying both the document and the property or thing.

The legal document you see must now "enter you" and convince you that the thing exists. You get that conviction by viewing or verifying its existence. Faith therefore has two parts:

a. A document part – substance – title deed.
b. A viewing/verifying part – evidence – inner conviction.

The legal aspect of faith is what is written in the bible. The viewing aspect, which gives you conviction in your heart that this written document is genuine, is the revelation you receive from God through His Word concerning the matter.

The following are three questions that help us to be convinced beyond every reasonable doubt about what we hope for:

1. Is it true?
Is it reliable in accordance with fact and reality?

2. Is it genuine?
    Is it truly what it is said to be without addition or subtraction?

3. Is it possible?
    Is it capable of existing, happening, or being achieved?

Faith is a Bridge

A bridge provides a link, connection, or means of coming together. Simply put, there must be faith between hope and the thing hoped for. There must be the substance of the thing. Once I have the faith, I have the basis of possessing my desire.

It is not so much about the desire, but the title deed (faith) that qualifies you to lay claim to the thing you desire or are praying for. The issue with Christians is that some cry to God for an expectation/hope but there is nothing to bridge the gap between that expectation/hope and the thing itself. They keep crying for expectation/hope without applying faith.

Believing

There must be something to lock down that expectation. Once you have that thing (faith, title deed) in your name, it is yours because you have the document that validates your claim to it.

How then do you lock down the expectation or the request you make in prayer? You do so by BELIEVING! When you pray, you must believe that you have RECEIVED IT.

Hope must be combined with faith, having something now that proves what you want. Once you have that legal paper, consider the thing you want GRANTED.

TEST YOUR UNDERSTANDING OF CHAPTER 12

1. When will the thing you pray for be yours?

2. What is the process of bringing a desire to fruition?

3. How do you classify a desire for money?

4. How do you classify a check of a certain amount of money in response to the need for money?

5. As you have the check, you have the substance of the money you were hoping for. True or False?

6. What are the three questions that help a person to be convinced about what he or she hopes for?

7. _____ becomes the basis of possession or ownership.

8. Hoping is possession. True or False?

9. Believing is receiving. True or False?

10. What is wrong with a believer crying for an expectation without results?

CHAPTER 13

Payment and Possession

"28 After this, Jesus knew that everything had been done. So that the Scripture would come true, he said, "I am thirsty." 30 When Jesus tasted the vinegar, he said, "It is finished." Then he bowed his head and died" (John 19:28, 30; NCV).

As we conclude, a major point to deal with in this subject of hope versus faith is about payment and possession. Payment is the settlement of a debt or other obligation. Possession is to have as belonging to one. The two are not the same. One is settlement of a debt. The other is having a belonging.

Scripture Has Been Fulfilled

All that needed to be done for the scriptures to be fulfilled has been done. When Jesus said, "I am thirsty", He was deliberately fulfilling scripture even at the time of death. Moreover, when He said, "It is finished", every price for the forgiveness of sin has been paid.

That is why it is recorded in Psalms 103 that He forgives all iniquities and heals all diseases. If Christ had not fully paid the price of sin, not all sins would have been forgiven. Then no one would have gained access to healing, or deliverance, or blessing.

Payment is Proof of Ownership

Whether natural or supernatural, temporary or eternal, spiritual or material, no one can acquire life. God, the creator of everything, is the giver of life.

On our behalf, Jesus has already paid for every blessing of God our Father. We only have to access them by faith. Thus, we should acknowledge our possession from the moment Christ paid and not when we see it.

Focus On the Time of Payment

In many cases, instead of focusing on Christ's payment of every debt of sin, Christians rather tend to focus on when they will physically possess the needs they pray for.

Imagine there is something you simply cannot afford. In fact, people cannot afford many things. If someone pays for that thing in your name, it is as if you paid for it yourself. As soon as payment is made, that thing is yours whether you go for it or not. The physical possession of the item paid for is initially not relevant because without the payment, there is nothing to possess anyway.

Do Not Pay Again

We need to keep saying, "I believe I've received so and so." For example, "by the stripes of Jesus Christ, I believe I have received my healing." Then we can say, "I'm healed" when we experience the manifestation of divine healing.

In John 19:30, Jesus screamed, "It is finished!" meaning, every price is paid. So do not pay for anything again." Your attention must be on the price our Lord Jesus has paid and maintain that confession. It is on that basis you have the right to enjoy the manifestation. You are the reason He suffered to pay the ultimate price.

TEST YOUR UNDERSTANDING OF CHAPTER 13

1. Which of the two expressions – possession and payment – comes first in order? And why?

2. What was Jesus doing when He said, "I am thirsty?"

3. What was Jesus inferring when He when He said, "It is finished?"

4. How is it possible for God to forgive all iniquities and heal all diseases?

5. Everything Jesus Christ did was on our behalf. True or False?

6. What does a believer stand to gain from Christ's fulfillment of scripture?

7. When is something yours? Is it when you have physical possession of it or when payment is made in your name?

8. When should I acknowledge my possession of God's promise?

9. Explain why the physical possession of an item paid for is initially irrelevant.

10. Where should a believer focus his or her attention and what should be his or her attitude?

Find the Answers to All the Questions

Find the Answers to the Questions in Chapter 1:
1. Three (3) Virtues
2. Faith, Hope, Charity or Love
3. Faith, Hope, Love (charity)
4. Love (charity)
5. The greatest
6. The greatest
7. Hebrews 11:1
8. Two (2)
9. Hope, Faith, Love (charity)
10. Write your own benefit here.

Find the Answers to the Questions in Chapter 2:
1. Hope is a joyful and confident expectation of a desired good based on what God has promised.
2. Desire and expectation
3. The feeling or emotion
4. The mind or mental part
5. When it is good and attainable
6. Yes

7. The other virtues must be set in motion for it to materialize.
8. It produces the strength of conviction to eliminate all doubt.
9. They sustain hope until its fulfillment.
10. Hope = Desire + Expectation or Confident Belief.

Find the Answers to the Questions in Chapter 3:

1. An anchor for the soul
2. Fleshly lusts.
3. It is because they are sojourners and pilgrims or strangers and travelers in the world, not citizens.
4. Which part of the human faculty is engaged in the war? The Soul
5. It is described as a ship on the sea.
6. The wind of false doctrines and wrong information.
7. It serves the twofold purpose of certainty and stability.
8. It requires a trustworthy promise.
9. True.
10. When a person's hope is in people and things and not in God

Find the Answers to the Questions in Chapter 4:

1. It is the substance of things hoped for and the evidence of things not seen.
2. They are, "substance"…"hoped for" and "evidence"
   …"not seen."
3. True.
4. It implies fully convincing a person to act in line with that conviction.
5. Faith = Belief + Action
6. False. He created the world by His word.
7. It takes faith.
8. Twice.
9. She naturally heard people's testimony about Him but later heard her inner spirit saying within herself.
10. She did first by meeting people who testified about Jesus and then by meditation or thinking of what she heard about Jesus.

Find the Answers to the Questions in Chapter 5:

1. The scripture or the written word.
2. The understanding or revelation you receive from God through His Word concerning the matter.
3. Author.

4. God
5. He created all things by His Word.
6. True
7. Jesus Christ
8. Exousia.
9. Those who believe in the Lordship of Jesus Christ. This is because, God fully grants all promises in Christ backed by all the honor of His Name.
10. He has authorized believers to act, make decisions, or allocate resources on His behalf or in His name.

Find the Answers to the Questions in Chapter 6:
1. The ability, strength, and capacity to do something.
2. Dunamis
3. Dynamite.
4. It represents a class of explosives used in mining or blasting.
5. True
6. It produces change and development consistent with the change and development it undergoes.
7. Those who believe are the ones who understand the scriptures.
8. The dynamic power that causes changes.

9. The word in the mind is inactive.
10. It is only when he or she meditates on it day and night and gets the true meaning that it begins to work forcefully.

Find the Answers to the Questions in Chapter 7:
1. The verse indicates their positions in a person.
2. A helmet is a hard protective piece of armor used for covering the head.
3. It represents hope.
4. A breastplate is a piece of armor that covers the chest, which is the region of the heart.
5. It represents faith and love.
6. The soul or the mind.
7. The spirit or the heart
8. The body or joints marrows.
9. One, and that is hope.
10. Two, and they are Faith and love.

Find the Answers to the Questions in Chapter 8:
1. They are not the same.
2. Belief begins with the mental acceptance of written facts.
3. Belief holds written facts as truth after a firm conviction in the heart.

4. Two parts.
5. The principle part and the practical part.
6. Faith = Belief + Action.
7. The principle or written part.
8. The practical part.
9. A person should believe what is written in the bible. He or she can do that by forming mental pictures of the words of the bible through meditation.
10. Jesus Christ our Lord.

Find the Answers to the Questions in Chapter 9:
1. 10.
2. Hope in the mind inspires confidence because there is an imminent expectation.
3. Faith in the heart generates joy and gladness because of the conviction of fulfillment.
4. We must be bold, firm, and consistent in declaring what we hope for to the end as if we already possess it.
5. Belief is part of both.
6. The mind bears the mental, intellectual and emotional burdens. The heart bears the spiritual burdens.
7. True.

8. Both are unseen; hence, they are eternal, having no beginning or end.
9. Every promise of God is fulfilled in Christ. All who believe in Christ inherit all things.
10. My personal benefit (s):

Find the Answers to the Questions in Chapter 10:
1. 4. Position, Period, Prospect, Perception
2. Position:
   Hope is located in the mind–mental.
   Faith is located in the heart–spiritual
3. Period:
   Hope is a period directed toward the unspecified future.
   Faith is the same hope considered as established now.
4. Prospect:
   Hope has the possibility of occurrence.
   Faith is actual occurrence.
5. False. A godly desire in the heart is faith, not hope.
6. False. A godly desire in the mind is hope, not faith.
7. True.
8. The future is a moment that is yet to come. The present is the moment when something is

currently happening, taking place or existing now.

9. It is because hope is not confined to a specified period.

10. Faith must deliberately change the period of hope from the future tense to the present or even the past tense.

Find the Answers to the Questions in Chapter 11:

1. The word of faith.

2. The word of hope.

3. God's faithfulness.

4. God's faith.

5. We hope for the appearing of our Lord Jesus Christ.

6. This event will culminate in the resurrection of the dead in Christ and the rapture of the saints.

7. God calls those things that are not as though they were.

8. It is always to exercise the God-kind of faith already possessed in Christ.

9. It is the language of hope.

10. "…you shall be a father/mother…" is the language of hope. "…I have made you a father/mother…" is the language of faith.

Find the Answers to the Questions in Chapter 12:
1. It is yours when you believe that you have received it.
2. Faith must be between hope and expectation.
3. Hope.
4. Faith.
5. True.
6. Is it true? Is it genuine? Is it possible?
7. Faith (substance, deed, or document).
8. False. Hope only brings awareness.
9. True. When you believe, then it is yours.
10. They do not convert hope to faith.

Find the Answers to the Questions in Chapter 13:
1. Payment comes first because acquisition leads to ownership or possession.
2. He was deliberately fulfilling scripture even at the time of death.
3. He had paid every debt of sin for it to be forgiven.
4. If Christ had not fully paid the price of sin, not all sins would have been forgiven. Then no one would have gained access to healing, or deliverance, or blessing.
5. True.

6. He or she has unlimited access to every blessing of God by faith.
7. When payment is made in your name.
8. From the moment Christ paid, not when I see it naturally.
9. There is nothing to possess unless payment is first made.
10. His or her attention must be on the price our Lord Jesus has paid and maintain that confession.

About the Author

Rev. Emil Elorm Clad is the Senior Pastor of the Christ Tower of Grace, an Apostolic Ministry committed to discipleship and raising of a prophetic generation around the globe. It is located along the Kwabenya-Brekusu road in Accra, Ghana.

He is an alumnus of the Torchbearer Bible School in Bodenseehof, Germany, and holds a diploma in Biblical Studies and Theology from the Victorious End Time Training Institute in Accra.

Rev. Clad authors the Faith Confession Aid; a compendium of daily faith declarations – currently available as an app on Google Play Store–which is empowering a growing movement of believers, teaching them to live victoriously by deploying the power of faith confession.

He has authored other books including,

"The Holy Spirit and Tongues: Benefits and Misuse."

"Finding Your Life Partner! A Personal Experience."

"The Mystery of Sex - Vol. 1."

Tamar's Transaction with Judah! An Example of Hope and Faith."

"The Place of Respect in Marriage."

He has been privileged to speak in nations in West Africa, Europe and North America.

He is married to Rev. (Mrs.) Erica Konadu Clad, and they are blessed with a son and three daughters.

Contact Information

Our ultimate desire is to publish the good news of God's grace. If you have been blessed by the message in this volume, share your testimony or benefits with us. Perhaps yours may be a question or concern. Do not hesitate to get in touch.

For Book Order, Bulk purchase or Speaking Engagements, please contact:

Emil Elorm Clad,
P. O. Box KN 683,
Kaneshie, Accra
Ghana

Email: emilclad@yahoo.com,
emil.clad.gh@gmail.com

Telephones:
+233 20 842 9790
+233 27 768 3706
+233 24 215 4928

www.ingramcontent.com/pod-product-compliance
Lightning Source LLC
Chambersburg PA
CBHW061747020426
42331CB00006B/1378